MARCO POLO

Retold by Kathy Reynolds

Illustrated by Daniel Woods

Raintree Childrens Books
Milwaukee
Belitha Press Limited • London

First published in the United States of America 1986
by Raintree Publishers Inc.
310 West Wisconsin Avenue, Milwaukee, Wisconsin 53203,
in association with Belitha Press Ltd, London.

Conceived, designed and produced by Belitha Press Ltd,
31 Newington Green, London N16 9PU

Cover printed in the United States; body printed by South China
Printing, Hong Kong; bound in the United States of America.

1 2 3 4 5 6 7 8 9   89 88 87 86

Library of Congress Cataloging in Publication Data
Reynolds, Kathy.
  Marco Polo.

  (Raintree stories)
  Summary: Recounts the adventures of the Italian
merchant during his travels to China, based on Marco
Polo's own accounts.
  1. Polo, Marco, 1254-1323?—Juvenile literature.
2. Explorers—Italy—Biography—Juvenile literature.
[1. Polo, Marco, 1254-1323? 2. Explorers] I. Woods,
Dan, ill. II. Polo, Marco, 1254-1323? Travels of
Marco Polo. III. Title.
G370.P9T75   1986   910'.92'4 [B] [92]   86-6678
ISBN 0-8172-2627-3 (lib. bdg.)
ISBN 0-8172-2635-4 (softcover)

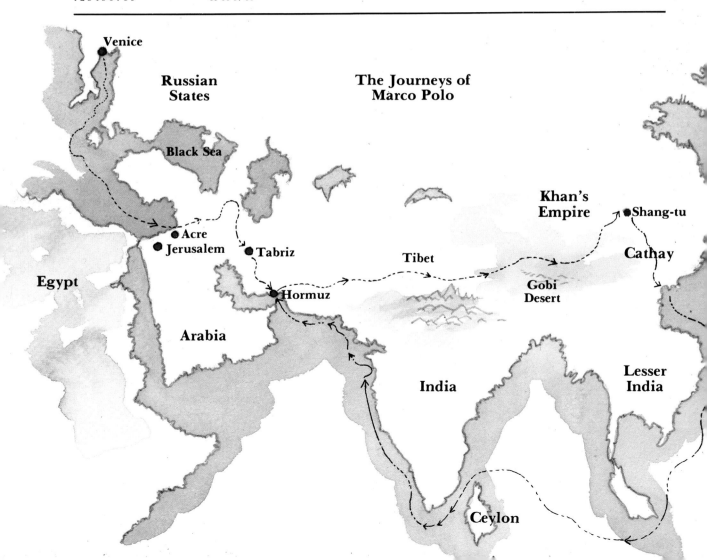

About seven hundred years ago, two great cities in Italy—Venice and Genoa—were at war. A Venetian ship was captured, and the captain, Marco Polo, was sent to prison in Genoa. There he met a writer called Rustichello. One day Marco told the writer about some strange adventures he had had in a faraway land. Rustichello said they should write a book about the journey. And so the story of the travels of Marco Polo began.

I was born in Venice. My father was a merchant, and just before I was born, he and my uncle went on a long journey to the East to buy goods. For years and years, we heard nothing. Then one day, they returned. I was fifteen.

They told us about going across the world to a country called Cathay. The people there, the Tartars, were ruled by a great and powerful man, Kublai Khan. The Khan was a curious man, eager to learn more about Western culture and religion. He sent my father and uncle home with a letter to the Pope, asking for a hundred wise men who could teach his people.

But when my father and uncle reached Venice, they learned there was no Pope. The old one had died, and a new one had not yet been chosen. They waited for two years. At last, afraid that any further delay would anger Kublai Khan, they decided to return to Cathay. I begged to go with them, and to my surprise and delight, they said I could. I was seventeen when we began our great adventure. Our journey was to last longer than any of us could have imagined.

We sailed first to the city of Acre in the Holy Land. The Khan had asked my father and uncle to bring back some holy oil from the lamp at the tomb of Christ in Jerusalem. It was believed to have magical powers. At Acre we met with Theobald, one of the most important priests in the Church of Rome. He arranged for us to get the holy oil.

We had gone on only as far as Ayas when word reached us that a new Pope had finally been elected. He was none other than our friend Theobald, now called Pope Gregory X. Of course, we returned to Acre. Even the Pope could not find a hundred wise men, but he ordered two learned friars to go with us. He also sent a message to the Khan, and costly gifts. Once again, we were on our way.

I soon discovered that traveling was not only exciting, but very dangerous. When we reached the kingdom of Armenia, there was a war going on. The two friars were frightened and decided to return home. My father, uncle and I continued our journey, but by a different route.

We swung far north into the kingdom of Georgia to avoid the war. Then we traveled south along the western shore of the Caspian Sea into Persia. We were headed for Hormuz, a seaport on the Persian Gulf. We had learned that from there it was possible to sail by ship, first to India and then to Cathay.

We traveled through hot, dry land. There was little grass, and water wells were far apart. Traders could find nothing to feed their pack animals. Large groups of bandits roved the countryside, killing and plundering. Merchants traveled in groups for safety.

At one place, not far from Hormuz, we were attacked by bandits called Karaunas. These fierce robbers were believed to have magical powers. They were said to be able to darken the day and create clouds of fog. Then they attacked their confused and frightened victims. I was almost captured in this way, but I escaped. Others in our group were not so lucky.

When we reached Hormuz, the heat was stifling. We were told that in summer, everyone left the city to escape the unhealthy air. Even the plants shriveled up in the heat. The fruits and vegetables were harvested by March.

We searched for a ship to take us to India, but we were dismayed at what we saw. The ships were very small and badly built. Instead of being fastened with iron nails, the planks were sown together with coconut-husk thread. The seams were caulked with fish oil, rather than pitch. We heard that many such ships had sunk in the Indian Ocean!

We decided to continue our journey by land. Once again we crossed arid desert. What little water we found often made us ill. When we did arrive at a spring of fresh water, or a town where we could rest, we were most thankful.

We headed north and east, at times wandering through beautiful plains and lush valleys. When at last we reached the province of Badakhshan, we stayed for some time. I had been ill for a whole year. But the pure mountain air at Badakhshan cured me.

When we left, we hiked through steep mountain passes. Finally, we reached the plain of Pamir, also known as the Roof of the World. The air was so cold and pure that no birds flew there. And I noticed our fires did not burn brightly.

From the plain of Pamir, the road sloped down. At last we came to a big city called Lop, right at the edge of the Gobi Desert. We rested there a week to prepare for our journey. We stocked up on food and water—enough to last thirty days. It took that long to cross the Great Desert at its narrowest point.

14

We heard stories of strange noises and evil spirits in the desert. Travelers were advised to stay close to one another. It was said that if a person strayed from his party, he would hear strange voices calling to him. If he followed the voices, he would become hopelessly lost.

Careful travelers tied bells to the necks of their pack animals. That way they could keep track of them at night and in the blowing sand. And each night, a sign was pounded into the sand, pointing the way of the next day's journey.

When we had finally crossed the Great Desert, we were in the lands ruled by Kublai Khan. Our travels had already lasted three and a half years.

When we arrived at the Khan's summer palace at Shang-tu, he gave us a warm welcome. He asked many questions about our journey. We presented him with his gifts, including the holy oil, which he received with much joy.

The Khan's summer palace was actually a huge tent. It was made of bamboo reeds, held together by silken ropes. Inside, it was richly and colorfully furnished. The tent was pitched in the middle of a beautiful parkland in which every kind of animal was kept, for the Khan was a great hunter.

We were well entertained at the palace by the Khan's magicians. They were able to send his drinking cup flying through the air to his outstretched hand!

The Khan had an even more impressive palace at Khan-balik, the capital of Cathay. It had magnificent marble staircases and walls of silver and gold. It was huge, with a hall big enough to seat six thousand people for dinner.

We saw many wonderful things while we lived in Cathay. There was a kind of mineral, called salamander, which was dug out of a hillside. It was pounded, then washed. The remaining fibers were spun into cloth which resisted fire completely.

Another thing that amazed me was that the people in Kublai Khan's realm used paper money instead of gold and silver. Different sizes of paper were worth different amounts. Each note was signed by certain officials and stamped with the Khan's seal. This paper money was used in trading, while all the gold and silver was kept in the Khan's treasury.

19

The Khan had a very clever way of getting messages from one part of his great kingdom to another. From the capital, roads went out to many of the provinces. At every twenty-five miles along these roads there was a posting station—more than ten thousand in all! At the stations, messengers on horseback could find overnight lodgings and fresh horses.

For urgent messages, special riders were used. When they neared a station, they would blow a horn to alert the stable hand to have a fresh horse waiting. By changing horses quickly and galloping on, one rider could cover up to three hundred miles a day in this way.

We had not been long at Kublai Khan's palace before I had learned to speak and write four of the Tartar languages. This impressed the Khan. He sent me out as a kind of ambassador to conduct official business for him in the provinces. While I was on these missions, I made a point of noticing interesting things about the customs of the people I visited. The Khan was most interested in hearing these details when I returned from my travels.

I was in the Khan's service for many years. As I traveled throughout his empire and to other countries, I saw many wonderful things.

In the western-most province, I first saw elephants used in battle. They were ridden by soldiers from the nearby country of Burma. The Burmese soldiers attacked a Tartar army, whose horses were so scared by the huge animals that they had to be taken into the woods and tied up. The brave Tartar archers fought and won that battle from the ground.

Later, Kublai Khan sent troops into Burma and captured it. When I visited there, I saw beautiful towers of silver and gold. From them, small bells hung, which tinkled when the wind blew. The towers were built as a monument to a former king. Because the Tartars respected other people's religions, the Khan's troops had left the beautiful towers unharmed.

The Khan collected all kinds of religious relics. He had heard that in Ceylon were a tooth and begging bowl that had belonged to Buddha. I was sent on a great sea voyage to get them.

We set sail from Amoy, the greatest port in Cathay. The ships there were large and well-suited to long ocean voyages.

We visited many islands, including Java, the spice center of the world. At Sumatra, I saw many strange things—including a tree that dripped wine and another whose trunk was full of flour.

When we arrived at the beautiful island of Ceylon, I was able to purchase the tooth and begging bowl for the Khan. There I saw the largest ruby in the world—but the king would not let me buy it for any price.

From Ceylon we crossed to India. At Maarbar, I saw divers bringing up large oyster shells from the bottom of the sea. Inside were beautiful pearls. Next we came to a land in India famous for its diamonds. They were located in a valley infested with poisonous snakes. To get the precious stones, people threw chunks of meat into the valley, to which the diamonds stuck. When great white eagles carried off the meat, people followed them to their nests to collect the diamonds.

When I returned from India, it seemed that at last the Khan might honor our request to go home to Venice. We had asked his permission before, but he had always refused. This is what happened to change his mind:

Kublai Khan's great-nephew, Arghun, was the ruler of Persia. His queen had died, and her last request had been that he would marry again from her family. So an embassy from Persia was sent to Cathay to bring back a new bride. A seventeen-year-old princess, Kokachin, was chosen. The party set off on the return trip to Persia by land. But after eight months they had to turn back. A Tartar war had broken out and it was not safe to continue by that route.

They turned back to ask Kublai Khan for help. Since I had just returned from my long voyage from India, they were most interested in the sea route I had taken. Finally, the Khan agreed to let my father, my uncle, and me escort the princess and her party to Persia. We were given a fleet of fourteen large ships, six hundred men, and food to last two years.

Our voyage was filled with danger—storms, pirates, and illnesses. After twenty-one months we reached Hormuz. Only eighteen of our crewmen were still alive!

We left the princess in Persia and continued on our way home. We trekked through Armenia, sailed across the Black Sea to Constantinople, and finally we reached Venice.

We had been gone twenty-three years, and our worn and stained Tartars' clothes made us look like tramps. It was no wonder that no one recognized us. So we prepared a great feast and invited family and old friends. We ripped the seams of our clothing apart and showered our guests with diamonds, rubies, and pearls—all the treasures we had brought back. After that, we were welcomed with great joy.

Many people did not believe the stories I told about the rich treasures I had seen in the East and the strange customs of the people there. I was nicknamed "Marco Millions" because they thought I told tall tales. But I swear to you that it is all true. There has never been a man yet who has explored so much of the world as I, Marco Polo, a citizen of Venice.